WRIGHTBUS
FROM 1946 TO NEW HORIZONS

KEITH A. JENKINSON

First published 2020

Amberley Publishing
The Hill, Stroud
Gloucestershire, GL5 4EP

www.amberley-books.com

Copyright © Keith A. Jenkinson, 2020

The right of Keith A. Jenkinson to be identified as the Author of this work has been asserted in accordance with the Copyright, Designs and Patents Act 1988.

ISBN 978 1 3981 0388 7 (print)
ISBN 978 1 3981 0389 4 (ebook)

All rights reserved. No part of this book may be reprinted or reproduced or utilised in any form or by any electronic, mechanical or other means, now known or hereafter invented, including photocopying and recording, or in any information storage or retrieval system, without the permission in writing from the Publishers.

British Library Cataloguing in Publication Data.
A catalogue record for this book is available from the British Library.

Typesetting by Aura Technology and Software Services, India. Printed in UK.

Introduction

Although the business which became known as Wrightbus was started by Robert Wright in 1946, it was not until the mid-1950s that the construction of bus bodies commenced, and the 1980s before the company became recognised as a serious manufacturer of large passenger-carrying vehicles. Since then, Wright's bodies – and later complete integrally built buses – have become familiar throughout the UK and in several overseas locations. However, due to financial difficulties, the bubble burst in 2019 when family owned Wrightbus was placed in administration and was ultimately sold to a new owner.

Without the help of several friends, it would have been extremely difficult to complete this history, and I am most grateful to them for their generosity in allowing me to use a number of their excellent photographs. All of these have been credited in the captions, and to those who are unfortunately unknown to me and thus credited as 'author's collection', I sincerely apologise, and hope that they will forgive me and enjoy seeing their work in print.

Wrightbus – from 1946 to Re-Birth

The history of Wrightbus dates back to 1946 when carpenter Robert Wright had emigrated to New Zealand in the early 1930s but had then returned to his native Ulster, where he set up a new joinery and house repairs business behind his house in Warden Street, Ballymena. After becoming established, in 1946 he was asked by the manager of the local Co-op if he could build a van body on a chassis scuttle, and after saying 'yes' and constructing this vehicle, he took the decision to diversify into vehicle bodybuilding and gradually phased out joinery and building work to give greater concentration to his new venture, which he named Robert Wright Coachworks Ltd.

Initially, the company concentrated on building van and wagon bodies on a variety of chassis, but then in the 1950s began constructing mobile shops, libraries, and ambulance bodies. Then, in the 1960s, after reaching an agreement with Telehoist, the company produced a range of skip and tipping lorries, trailers for articulated lorries, and demountable van bodies. Continuing to seek expansion, the company also entered into a contract with Short's Armoured Division to build a range of vehicles, such as Shorland armoured personnel carriers and missile launchers on Land Rover chassis.

Robert Wright Coachworks' first venture into more conventional passenger-carrying vehicles came in the mid-1950s when it began to produce a range of school bus bodies on Bedford, Commer, and Leyland chassis. These were for various County Education and Libraries Boards in Northern Ireland, and additionally as staff buses for local employer Michelin, whose factory was also in Ballymena. From these small acorns, on 17 September 1964 the company was renamed Robert Wright & Son (Coachbuilders) Ltd and continued its development of bus bodies for Regional Councils, Health Boards and Community Transport Associations in Scotland and England. By the 1980s it had become a major player in these markets.

After gaining a licensing agreement with Alusuisse in 1978, which enabled it to use its aluminium extrusions, in 1981 the company produced its first full size passenger-carrying vehicles when Ulsterbus ordered bodies on two 11m Leyland Leopard PSU3E/4R chassis. One was designated the TT model and was fitted with fifty-three bus seats, while the other, christened the Royal, an enhanced version of the TT, was more luxurious and equipped with fifty-three coach seats. Meanwhile, after forming Wrights Coachworks (Scotland) Ltd on 13 April 1981, the company opened a small satellite factory in Wishaw, Scotland, to support its Scottish and English customers with major accident damage repairs. However, finding this to have insufficient space for its needs, it soon moved to larger premises in Coatbridge, but unfortunately, after experiencing a number of burglaries in which substantial equipment and tooling was stolen, the factory was ultimately closed in 1986.

Having now built two full-size single-deckers, in November 1982 Robert Wright Coachworks introduced a new coach model which was given the name Contour. Like the TT and Royal, this used the Alusuisse method of construction and featured a stylish raked front with a single-piece curved windscreen. Although offered in varying lengths between 8.5m and 12m on ACE Puma, Bedford YMP, YMQ, YNT, Ford R1115, Leyland Tiger, and Volvo B10M chassis, only thirty-six Contours were built before the model was discontinued in 1987.

Towards the end of the 1980s, seeing the growing interest in small capacity vehicles, Robert Wright Coachworks turned its attention to the construction of midibuses on Mercedes Benz 709D and 811D, and Renault S75 chassis/scuttles, giving these the name Nimbus. Seating twenty-six/twenty-eight passengers, and like all future Wright bodies using Alusuisse construction, these were functional buses of pleasing appearance and attracted large orders from London Buses, Ulsterbus, and Dublin Bus, as well as numerous other operators, and remained available until July 1996. Then, on the morning of Friday 23 November 1989, disaster struck when fire destroyed a large part of the main building of the South Factory on Cushendall Road. Fortunately, however, although much of the building was gutted, most of the chassis and part-built midibuses were dragged out and saved, and production was able to continue in the North Factory, which escaped the blaze.

The next new model to be introduced was the Handybus on the Dennis Dart chassis. This had a no frills box-like design which lacked curves and was offered in 8.5m, 9m, and 9.8m lengths with seating for twenty-eight/forty passengers. It was available with a single-piece flat windscreen or twin flat windscreens, the latter of which was raked back on the driver's side. Making its debut in November 1990, it remained in production until March 1995, by which time just over 300 had been built.

Now turning its attention again to full-size, heavy duty single-deckers, in June 1992 the Endeavour body mounted on Leyland Tiger chassis was introduced for Ulsterbus. This had fifty-three dual purpose seats, high, shallow side windows, and a newly designed front, which was to become a feature of Wright bodies for several years. In addition, Yorkshire Traction also ordered Endeavour bodies, albeit on five Scania K93CRB chassis in August 1993, although these had fifty-three bus seats and deeper side windows.

Then, in August 1993, Wrights introduced its Cityranger body which was mounted on the Mercedes Benz 0405 chassis. Although it was structurally similar to the Endurance, which made its debut two months later, it featured a standard Mercedes Benz 0405 front and had shallower side windows. Only twenty-two were built, all but two of which began life in Scotland with Grampian and Midland Bluebird, with the final example being delivered in March 1994. As stated earlier, in October 1993 the company launched the Endurance, which was a step entrance body of an attractive design mounted on Volvo B10B and Scania N113 chassis. Available with seating for forty-nine/fifty-one passengers, it remained in production until 1997, during which time 318 had been built.

Following the Endurance was the low floor Pathfinder 320, which was available in single and dual-door format and was based on Dennis Lance SLF and Scania N113CRL chassis, both of which were 12m in length. Introduced in December 1993, it remained available until 1995 during which time ninety-five had been built. Then, another model using Endurance styling, but mounted on an 11.5m Mercedes Benz OH1416 chassis, was the forty-seven-seat Urbanranger, which appeared in July 1994. However, despite remaining on offer until April 1998, only sixteen were built.

Maintaining its recent predecessors body styling, the 12m Axcess Ultra Low on the Scania N113CRL chassis was introduced in March 1995 as a replacement for the Pathfinder and Endurance models. 330 were built before it was succeeded by the Axcess Floline in 1998. Then, following in August 1995 was the Crusader, which replaced the Handybus and used Dennis Dart SLF and Volvo B6 (and from 1996, Volvo B6LE) chassis. Available in 8.8m, 9.4m, 10.2m and 10.8m length, it used the same frontal styling as the Axcess Ultra Low but had side windows of a greater height and a shallow roofline. Proving to be a popular model, 425 were built, including twenty-six on Dennis Dart chassis for an Australian customer. It was, in 1999, replaced by the Crusader 2, which featured a deeper roof and shallower side windows and was mounted on the Volvo B6LE chassis. 262 were built.

In June 1996, Wrights began building bodies on the Volvo B10L chassis, this employing the same styling as the Axcess Ultra Low. Named Liberator, and offered with seating for up to forty-seven passengers, it was only built in single-door configuration except for eleven thirty-nine seaters that were dual-door and supplied to Dublin Bus. Never a best seller, however, only 143 were built before it was discontinued in December 1999.

Then, replacing the Endurance, in October 1997, was the Renown, which was mounted on the Volvo B10BLE chassis and largely retained the styling of its predecessor. Continuing in production until June 2002, during which time over 800 had been built, it had seating for thirty-nine/forty-one passengers and was available in single or dual-door format.

As stated earlier, the Axcess Floline, which was mounted on a Scania L94UB chassis and introduced in March 1998, replaced the almost identical Axcess Ultra Low. Except for eleven built in dual-door format for operation at London's Heathrow Airport, all the other 265 constructed until May 2001 were single-door and maintained the Ultra Low design. Then, later that year in October, Wrights launched its first bendy buses, these being based on Volvo B10LA chassis. Given the name Fusion, and using the same styling as the Axcess Floline, only forty were built – all for First Group companies – before production ended in November 1999.

Later, in October 1998, Wright began experimenting with hybrid electric propulsion, and thus equipped a prototype with single-door Crusader bodywork on a Dennis Dart SLF chassis. After further development, in September 2002 a second prototype was constructed using a DAF SB120 chassis and a Cadet body, albeit with dual doors. Both these assisted in further development of hybrid-electric technology, as will be seen later.

On 9 September 1999, Wright Group Ltd was formed as the parent company of all the Wright family controlled companies located at Galgorm, Ballymena. On 18 June 2000 Wrightbus Ltd was incorporated to bring together all its operations. Amongst these was Customcare, which had been incorporated on 12 May 1999 and provided aftermarket support, and Expotech, which had been created on 29 March 1999 as a launch platform for new business opportunities.

In April 2000, Wright introduced its Eclipse model, which featured a large one-piece windscreen with a curved base line and looked not dissimilar to the Nokia mobile phone. The first examples were Eclipse Fusion bendybuses, based on Volvo B7LA chassis, of which eighty-eight were built until December 2005.

Also using the Nokia-style windscreen was the Opus midibus, which was designed and developed by Expotech for the North American market. Built from 2000 to 2006 on a rear-engined chassis, it was developed by Opus Coach in Wichita, Kansas. After the first two bodies were built at Ballymena, all those that followed, some being 30 feet and others 35 feet long, were supplied in ckd form for assembly in Wichita.

Making its debut in May 2000 was the Cadet, which was based on the DAF SB120 chassis and could accommodate between twenty-eight and forty-two seats. Available in single or dual-door configuration, it continued Wright's well-established pre-Eclipse body design and remained in production until February 2008, during which time 681 had been built. After discontinuing its B6BLE chassis in 2002, Volvo then marketed the Wright-bodied VDL SB120 under the name Merit, which was completely devoid of any Wright, DAF, VDL or Volvo branding, continuing this until October 2006.

Returning to the design featuring the Nokia-style windscreen, and almost identical to the Eclipse, was the Solar, which was introduced in February 2001 on the 12m Scania L94UB chassis and later on its successor, the K230UB. At this same time, a bendy bus variant, named the Solar Fusion, was built on a Scania L94UA chassis, but only eleven were constructed.

In July 2001, Wright made its first entry into the double-deck bus market when it launched its Eclipse Gemini on a Volvo B7TL chassis. Featuring a Nokia-style windscreen and single-piece upper deck front bulkhead window front, it was of dual-door layout with seating for sixty-four passengers. It was initially supplied to the London bus market. After a single-door variant was built as a demonstrator in August 2002, production of this version commenced in June 2003, after which the Eclipse Gemini became a familiar sight across the UK. Then, in 2007, following minor face lifting at the rear to become the Eclipse Gemini 2, it was mounted on the Volvo B9TL chassis, which had replaced the B7TL. Turning to the export market, in March 2003 Wright began building eighty-seat dual-door Eclipse Geminis, designated Wright Explorer, on Volvo's tri-axle Super Olympian B10TL chassis for Kowloon Motor Bus, Hong Kong, then, from 2005, on its replacement, the Volvo tri-axle Super Olympian B9TL. Expanding its overseas market, in 2010 it supplied Eclipse Gemini dual-door bodies on tri-axle Volvo B9TLs to SMS Transit in Singapore.

Next to be built by Wright was the Commander, which mounted on a VDL SB200 chassis and was basically a 12m version of the Cadet, which retained its classic pre-Nokia Eclipse styling. Produced from March 2002 until the autumn of 2007, 315 were built including 191 left-hand drive examples for Arriva Netherlands.

Perpetuating the new Nokia style front was the Eclipse Urban, which was almost identical to the Solar, but was based on the 12m Volvo B7BLE chassis, first appearing in April 2003. In April 2004, an additional version of the Eclipse was introduced. This was the Eclipse Commuter, which used the Volvo B7RLE chassis but had the higher floor section extended to the front axle to allow under-floor storage and a higher seating position, while maintaining a small low floor area at the front for wheelchair passengers. Only four were built, however, with the last entering service in December 2005. Then, in 2006 the Eclipse SchoolBus was launched specifically for Ulsterbus, who took all the 160 built before it was discontinued in 2008. This was an entirely high floor version of the Eclipse Commuter and was mounted on the Volvo B7R coach chassis. Seating was provided for sixty-six passengers in a 2+3 layout. Meanwhile, the Eclipse Urban continued in production, being facelifted to match the StreetCar and renamed Eclipse 2 in November 2008. It was then mounted on the Volvo B8RLE chassis (successor to the B7RLE) to become the Eclipse 3 in June 2015. 11.8m and 13.2m variants were added to the range in April 2017 when the body was also offered with an Eclipse Gemini 3 Stealth windscreen.

In June 2003, Wright launched its Eclipse Gemini double-deck body on the VDL DB250 chassis, giving this the name Pulsar Gemini. Originally built in dual-door format, in May 2005 it was also offered with a single door and seating for sixty-seven passengers. The Pulsar Gemini remained in production until October 2006 by which time 189 had been built. In addition, between October 2006 and 2009, three VDL DB250 Pulsar Geminis were built as hybrid vehicles for in service testing.

Then, moving forward to 2004, in conjunction with FirstGroup and Volvo, Wrightbus designed and built a new articulated single-decker on the Volvo B7LA chassis. Named the StreetCar by Wright, and ftr (text speak for 'future of travel') by FirstGroup, it was built to have the appearance of a tram and had a separate cab for the driver. Of 18.7m length and 3.5m height, it accommodated forty-one seated and sixty-seven standing passengers and was fully air-conditioned. Only thirty-nine were built – all for FirstGroup – the last being placed in service in October 2007. In addition to these, Wright built fifty left-hand drive StreetCars on Carrosserie Hess chassis for RTV Transit, Southern Nevada, USA, in 2008/9.

On 7 September 2005, Wright Group created another new division, Wright Composites Ltd, to produce glass reinforced plastic (GRP) componentry for Wrightbus and outside customers.

Continuing to develop alternative propulsion, in December 2005 Wright introduced a new version of its single-deck Electrocity, which was based on the VDL SB120 chassis. It had lead-acid batteries mounted on its roof and was fitted with a 1.9 litre Vauxhall engine. Six of these buses, all of which were of dual-door configuration, were placed in service by London Central for a long-term trial. In 2011 all were returned to Ballymena to be fitted with lithium-ion batteries and a 4.5 litre Cummins engine before being returned to London. Then, between November 2007 and October 2011, a further fifteen Electrocitys were built, all with dual-door bodies, again for operation in London.

Replacing the Commander in November 2006 was the Pulsar, a 12m model similar to the Eclipse, but built on the VDL SB200 chassis. After 114 had been built, in March 2009 it was slightly facelifted and re-designated Pulsar 2, of which 525 were built before it was finally discontinued in April 2014.

In March 2007, Wrightbus launched a new semi-integrally constructed double-decker based on VDL DB300 modules. It was named the Wright Gemini 2DL when fitted with a Cummins 6-cylinder diesel engine and the Wright Gemini 2HEV when equipped as a diesel-electric hybrid with a Ford Sigma engine. Based on the Eclipse Gemini body design, it was available in dual and single-door configuration and, in addition, a low-height variant with a flat roof was offered. However, only thirteen HEVs were built, all for operation in London, the last of which entered service in April 2009, while the 462 DLs were constructed between January 2009 and September 2013.

The first MAN chassis to be bodied by Wright were NL273Fs (A22) which made their debut in November 2007. Using Eclipse-style bodies but given the name Meridian, only twenty-eight were built, however, with the last taking up its duties in February 2011.

In a bid to compete with the Optare Solo SR and Versa, in July 2010 a new integrally built rear-engined midibus named the StreetLite was introduced. Initially it was offered in 8.8m and 9.5m lengths as the StreetLite WF (wheel-forward) with seating for thirty-three/thirty-nine passengers and the entrance door behind the front axle. Then, as not all operators were happy with this configuration, a second version – the StreetLite DF (door-forward) – was added in January 2012. This was available in 10.2m and 10.8m lengths and had the front axle set back to allow the door to be directly opposite the driver. Following on, in 2012, a longer 11.5m version of the DF was launched, this being given the name StreetLite Max. Then two years later, a left-hand drive WF variant made its debut, marketed by VDL as the Citea MLE. Only eleven were built, however, and all were sold to Danish and Dutch operators with the last being placed in service in June 2015. Continuing to look towards new forms of technology, in 2013 Wright introduced a hybrid version of the StreetLite. Named the StreetLite Micro Hybrid and available in all of the StreetLite lengths, it was, however, not a hybrid (in the usual sense). It featured a conventional diesel engine and recovered energy lost from braking to power its electrics and compressed air systems. Following these, in 2014 the Streetlite DF and WF were also made available as full hybrid-electric vehicles. In January 2014 the DF was additionally trialled as a full electric bus with no diesel engine, and used inductive charging. Then, added to the range in 2015 was the StreetVibe, which was a WF model built by Nu Track (of which more later) to a design similar to the StreetLite. Of 9m length, it was of a narrower width than the standard StreetLite, thus making it suitable for operation in rural areas.

Meanwhile, on 23 December 2009, Wrightbus won the contract to build a new double-deck bus for Transport for London. Designed by London-based Heatherwick Studio, it was a futuristic design of 11.2m length, with seating for sixty-two passengers, three doors, and two staircases, both of which featured a glazed panel running from the lower to upper deck. Integrally constructed, it was a hybrid diesel-electric with a Cummins 4-cylinder, 4.5 litre engine. After a mock-up had been built, the first genuine example was unveiled in December 2011 and entered service in February 2012. It was joined by a further seven over the next five months before full delivery commenced in the early summer of 2013. A total of 1,000 were built, with the final examples taking up their duties in December 2017. Had it not been for the decision of the new Mayor of London, who cancelled further orders, many more would undoubtedly have been built.

On 1 March 2011, Wrightbus created a new subsidiary, Metallix, to manufacture the metal structures, and parts of structures, for use in its bus construction.

Following this, in December 2012 Wrightbus set up yet another new subsidiary, EN Drive, on the Newpark Industrial Estate on the outskirts of Antrim, which became the new chassis design and manufacturing arm for Wright's integral buses, but could also provide chassis to external customers.

On 20 November 2012, Antrim-based Nu-Track became loosely associated with the Wright Group when it was purchased by Jeff Wright, majority shareholder in the Wright Group and owner of its Galgorm factory. Nu-Track had commenced in business in October 1991, building minibus conversions, welfare and school buses, horseboxes, and mobile libraries. Following its change of ownership in 2012, despite moving its registered address to that of Wrightbus, Nu-Track remains a private limited company, building a wide range of vehicles under its own name.

Also, in 2012, in order to spread its wings further afield, Wrightbus International was created largely to solicit orders from Hong Kong and Malaysia, where double-deck buses were in constant demand. Later, in 2014, Wrightbus International entered into an agreement with Comfort Delgro Engineering, in Singapore, to assemble buses supplied in ckd form from Ballymena.

Returning to Wright's conventional double-deckers, in 2013 the Eclipse Gemini was given a further facelift when it was given shallower upper deck side windows in a bid to save weight and was designated the Gemini 3. Then, in July 2015 it was further changed when it was given a new frontal design, nicknamed 'Stealth', which featured a different shaped windscreen and upper deck bulkhead window and thick unglazed upper deck front corner pillars. It was offered with a glazed staircase panel as well as in part open-top format. The pre-Stealth variant was still, however, available into 2019 on the Volvo B5TL and Volvo B5LH chassis.

Then, in November 2014 came the StreetDeck, a 10.6m integrally constructed low-floor double-decker, the first five of which were fitted with a front similar in appearance to the Gemini 2. However, when general production commenced in February 2015, these were given the new 'Stealth' design body, which was offered with single or dual doors and with or without a glazed staircase. The engine used was a Daimler 5.1 litre, 4-cylinder Euro 6 diesel engine. In addition, a variant was made available using the same Micro Hybrid technology as the StreetLite. In May 2018 a full hybrid-electric version was added to the StreetDeck range. Meanwhile, at the request of several operators, to enhance front upper deck visibility, glazing was added to the thick front upper deck corner pillars for those who preferred it. Over 700 StreetDecks had been built by September 2019 when Wrightbus went into administration. In addition, seven left-hand drive, dual-door StreetDecks were built – five for Monterey, California, in October 2017, and one each for Hong Kong and San Diego in 2019.

In November 2016, Wrightbus built a body closely resembling the New Bus for London on a Volvo B5LH chassis, this being 10.5m in length with two doors and one staircase. Following this, in June 2018, it built two similar bodies on the electric version of the Volvo B5LHC, both of which had conductive pantograph charging on their roof.

Finally, in February 2017 Wrightbus launched a new low-floor all-electric integrally constructed single-deck model, designated the StreetAir, as a replacement for the Electrocity and StreetLite EV. Offered with either single or dual doors, the StreetAir's battery pack is mounted full length on its roof. To date only eight have been built, six of which were for Lothian Buses in September 2017.

Sadly, in September 2019, due to a downturn in the UK bus market, Wrightbus urgently sought a cash injection of around £30 million in order to be able to stay in business. Failing to achieve that and unable to find a buyer for the company, it was placed into administration on 25 September 2019 with a loss of 1,145 jobs. Despite engaging in talks with several parties, all to no avail, and tottering on the brink of extinction, after selling Wrights Composites to Peter Drayne, a Lisburn investor, on 11 October, twelve days later Ryse Hydrogen owner Jo Bamford, grandson of JCB founder Joseph Bamford, clinched a deal to purchase the factory and business of the Northern Ireland coachbuilder after registering a new company, Bamford Bus Company Ltd, for this purpose. Prior to the collapse of Wrightbus, Ryse Hydrogen had, however, already been working with the company on the twenty hydrogen-powered double-deckers ordered by Transport for London. Thus, the future of Wrightbus looks to have been secured, although in which direction the company will continue, in respect of its current model range, is not known at the time of writing.

Had it not been for Wrightbus's failure, further StreetAirs in development would have resulted in double-deckers being built with electricity conduction via overnight (plug in), and inductive (through the road surface) methods, as well as single-deckers with a conductive pantograph.

After entering administration, all Wrightbus's part-built buses, and those completed that were awaiting delivery to their new owners, were mothballed until the company's future was assessed, and it was not until after it had been purchased by Bamford Bus Company Ltd that deliveries recommenced. The first buses to leave Ballymena were part of a fifty-five-bus StreetDeck order for First Leeds, which, after being impounded by the administrator, began to depart on 7 November. At around the same time, some work within the factory restarted with a small skeleton staff. Meanwhile, preparing for the future, recruiting new skilled employees had begun. However, this was believed to be around 500 and not in the numbers of those that had been made redundant. The production line is planned to be running again by February 2020, and the future of the company now looks secure. Meanwhile, Wrightbus International, which was not included in the administration, continued to trade independently, although it is thought that it too might ultimately be acquired by Bamford Bus Company.

Having been family owned for almost seventy-five years, and always based in Ballymena, Northern Ireland, Wrightbus is now set to move forward under its new ownership, and will no doubt continue to be an innovative company embracing new technology as it had done in the past. Its buses will, however, continue to be branded with the Wrightbus name despite Wrightbus Ltd being renamed WB 2019 Realisations Ltd on 16 November 2019.

The first vehicle built by Robert Wright was this Austin van for Ballymena & Harryville Co-op, which he constructed in 1946. (Wrightbus)

Former military Bedford TK GDZ 7756, which was new in February 1979, was given its new tipping body by Robert Wright Coachworks in 1989. (K. A. Jenkinson)

Built by Robert Wright Coachworks in November 1985 as a mobile library on a Bedford VAS3 chassis is ADZ 3247, which was supplied new to the th East Education & Library Board at Ballymena. (K. A. Jenkinson)

Fitted with a Robert Wright Coachworks flat platform body is Freight Rover Sherpa FXI 6033. (K. A. Jenkinson)

Supplied new to the Western Education and Library Board in October 1978 was fifty-three-seat Wright-bodied Albion Viking EJI 401, which featured a peaked front roof dome. (Will Hughes)

New in 1981 was Wright Royal-bodied Leyland Leopard AXI 2259, which was supplied to Ulsterbus as its number 259, and is seen here at Larne on 10 September 1989. (K. A. Jenkinson)

In 1984 Wright built twenty-five buses on Bedford chassis, with bodies based on its TT design, for export to Federated Motor Industries in Africa. (Wrightbus)

Built in May 1985 as a school bus for Northern Ireland's Southern Education and Library Board is Dodge S50 HIB 9430. (Will Hughes)

Mounted on a rare Ace Puma chassis in May 1985 is this thirty-five-seat Contour body for coach operator Abbeyways of Halifax, who registered it B938 BVH. (John Law)

Also new in May 1985 was Ulsterbus 537 (GXI 537), a forty-nine-seat Contour-bodied Leyland Tiger, which is seen here at Newry on 10 September 1989. (K. A. Jenkinson)

Although many of the mobile shop bodies were built by Wright on Bedford chassis, IIL 2734, which is now preserved, is mounted on a Karrier chassis. (Wrightbus)

Given a twelve-seat Wright body, Flexibus 6 (GXI 5006) is a Mercedes Benz 307D, which was new in September 1985 and is seen here at Larne depot on 6 September 1992. (K. A. Jenkinson)

Built by Wright on a Land Rover chassis for Shorland was this S52 armoured car. (Wrightbus)

Amongst the numerous school buses built for Northern Ireland Education and Libraries Boards was TT-bodied Bedford YMT KJI 1739, which was new in May 1987. (Will Hughes)

Built as a mobile library in January 1989, but seen here in use as a mobile shop, is FIL 6601, a Leyland Swift with a Wright body based on the TT design. (Author's collection)

In the 1970s and 1980s, Wright built a number of ambulances on Ford Transit chassis/scuttles including now preserved DIA 1979, seen here restored to its original glory. (Author's collection)

Displaying Busy Bus identity and standing outside Larne depot on 10 September 1989 is twenty-five-seat Ulsterbus Wright-bodied Mercedes Benz 709D 829 (NXI 6829), which was new in February of that year. (K. A. Jenkinson)

Seen at Great Victoria Street depot, Belfast, on 6 September 1992, with Airbus branding, is Ulsterbus 1809 (SXI 2809), a coach-seated Wright-bodied Mercedes Benz 811D that began life in June 1990. (K. A. Jenkinson)

Fitted with a single-piece windscreen, twenty-nine-seat Wright Handybus-bodied Dennis Dart K985 CBO began life with London Buses in February 1993 registered NDZ 3140. It was later operated by Stagecoach Red & White before being acquired by Halifax Joint Committee, with whom it is seen here at Brighouse Tesco. (K. A. Jenkinson)

Wearing Westlink livery, Wright Handybus-bodied Dennis Dart DWL6 (JDZ 2406), which was new to London Buses in December 1990, features twin windscreens with that on the offside being raked inwards. (Author's collection)

New to Ulsterbus in June 1992, high-floor dual-purpose fifty-three-seat Wright Endeavour-bodied Leyland Tiger WXI 4417 is seen here in Londonderry bus station, in July 2009, after its sale to Londonderry & Lough Swilly Railway Co. (K. A. Jenkinson)

Using a combination of body styles and built in February 1991, H365 AMT was a Dennis Javelin supplied to the London Borough of Havering for use as a school bus. (D. W. Rhodes)

One of five fifty-three-seat bus specification Wright Endeavour-bodied Scania K93CRBs with deeper side windows, purchased by Yorkshire Traction in August 1993, is K275 EWA, seen here at Waterloo depot, Huddersfield, on 6 March 2007. It is still wearing its original owner's livery after passing to Stagecoach with the Tracky business. (K. A. Jenkinson)

New to London United in December 1993, dual-door Wright Pathfinder-bodied Dennis Lance SLF ODZ 8906 later found a new home with West Midlands independent A2Z, with whom it is seen here at Walsall in October 2007. (K. A. Jenkinson)

Resting at Ulsterbus's Larne depot, on 14 September 1995, are two Busy Bus-branded Mercedes Benz 709Ds with different styles of Wright twenty-five-seat bodywork. 888 (AAZ 8888) was new in June 1993, while 830 (NXI 6830) began life in February 1989. (K. A. Jenkinson)

Fitted with a Wright forty-seat Handybus body, and new to Gateshead & District in February 1993, Dennis Dart K382 RTY is seen here in May 2007 after being acquired by short-lived Knottingley independent South Yorkshire Motors. (K. A. Jenkinson)

One of a large number of Wright Nimbus-bodied Mercedes Benz 811Ds purchased by London Buses is NDZ 7931, which was new in April 1993. It is seen here at dealer Stafford Bus Centre after serving with several other operators since it left the capital. (K. A. Jenkinson)

Forty-seven-seat Wright Urban Ranger-bodied Mercedes Benz OH1416 L610 OWB began life as a demonstrator in July 1994, and later served with South Lancs Travel and West Midlands independent Choice Travel. (Author's collection)

Seen here with Stevensons, in Uttoxeter, is prototype Wright Cityranger-bodied Mercedes Benz 0405 L100 SBS, which incorporated a standard Mercedes Benz style front and was new in August 1993. (Will Hughes collection)

Supplied, when new in April 1995, to Northern Ireland's Western Education and Library Board, is Wright Urbanranger-bodied Mercedes Benz OH1416 1381 (TJI 4143). (Will Hughes)

Parked in the yard of its owner Midland Bluebird's Larbert depot, in September 1997, is Wright Endurance-bodied Scania N113CRB 565 (L565 JLS), which was new in July 1994. (K. A. Jenkinson)

Resting outside the Kirkstall depot of its owner, First Leeds, in September 2007, is Wright Axcess Ultra Low-bodied Scania L113CRL 62117 (N412 ENW), which was new to Rider York in September 1995. (K. A. Jenkinson)

Seen here in Barnsley, operated by Tate's Travel, is thirty-eight-seat Wright Crusader-bodied Volvo B6LE N416 KPS with deep side windows and shallow roof. New in November 1995, it began life on Shetland and later served with Stagecoach Merseyside. (K. A. Jenkinson)

Seen here at a Wrightbus celebratory event is Dennis Dart SLF VDZ 8001 fitted with a thirty-two-seat Wright Crusader body with deeper roof. New in September 1996, it was first operated by London United, by whom it was numbered CD1. (K. A. Jenkinson)

Leaving Buchanan bus station, Glasgow, is First Greater Glasgow Wright Liberator-bodied Volvo B10L SV560 (P762 XHS), which began life in May 1997 and displays First Express branding on its front panel. (K. A. Jenkinson)

With a Wright Crusader thirty-seven-seat body mounted on a Volvo B6LE chassis, Travel West Midlands 559 (P559 LDA), which was new in April 1997, is seen here in Walsall bus station on 11 November 2007. (K. A. Jenkinson)

New to University Bus, Hatfield, in September 1997, was Wright Crusader-bodied Dennis Dart SLF R654 VBM, seen here in St Albans. (T. W. W. Knowles)

Carrying a First Greater Glasgow fleet name, and seen here in September 1997 when only four weeks old, is Wright Axcess Ultra Low-bodied Scania L113CRL SS15 (R115 GSF), which had seating for forty passengers. (K. A. Jenkinson)

Seen on demonstration at First Bradford's depot is Wright's prototype Electrocity AKZ 7122, a Crusader-bodied hybrid electric bus built in October 1998 on a Dennis Dart SLF chassis. (K. A. Jenkinson)

Exhibited at a bus and coach show at the NEC, Birmingham, in October 1998, is a Wrightbus Axcess Floline-bodied Scania L94UB in the livery of First Greater Glasgow. As can be seen, its body styling was almost identical to the Axcess Ultra Low, which it replaced. (K. A. Jenkinson)

The first bendy buses built by Wright were Fusion-bodied Volvo B10LAs, one of which – First Glasgow 10110 (V610 GGB) – was new in December 1999 and is seen in its home city. (D. W. Rhodes)

On its way from Leeds Bradford airport to its hometown is Transdev Harrogate & District's Wright Crusader-bodied Volvo B6BLE 615 (W615 CWX), which was new in June 2000. (K. A. Jenkinson)

Leaving Huddersfield bus station is K-Line's thirty-nine-seat Wright Cadet-bodied DAF SB120 YJ51 ELO, which was new in September 2001, and was originally owned by Stephenson, Easingwold. (K. A. Jenkinson)

Three unidentified single-deckers are seen here under construction in Wright's Ballymena factory in October 1996. (K. A. Jenkinson)

Fitted with a Wright Eclipse Fusion body, Dublin Bus Volvo B7LA AW2 (OO-D-65002), which was new in April 2001, is seen eighteen months later resting in the yard of Broadstone depot. (K. A. Jenkinson)

Turning into Canal Street, near the city's Broadmarsh bus station, is Nottingham City Transport Wright Solar Fusion-bodied Scania L94UA bendy bus 702 (FP51 EXN), which was purchased new in November 2001. (K. A. Jenkinson)

New in April 2002 as a Volvo demonstrator, thirty-five-seat Wrightbus Eclipse Metro-bodied Volvo B7L LF02 PVA is seen here in Dartford after being added to the fleet of Arriva Kent & Surrey, by whom it was numbered 3730. (D. W. Rhodes)

Amongst the first Wrightbus Eclipse Gemini double-deckers to be built was Go London Central's dual-door Volvo B7TL VWL6 (LB02 YXD), which entered service in August 2002. It is seen here passing through Charlton en route to Belvedere Industrial Area on route 180. (K. A. Jenkinson)

Traversing Upper Queen Street, Belfast, in March 2011 is Translink Ulsterbus Wright Renown-bodied Volvo B10BLE 2803 (BCZ 2803), which was new in May 2000. (Paul Savage)

A second Wrightbus Electrocity demonstrator to be examined by First Bradford was Cadet-bodied DAF SB120 YG52 CCX, which was new in September 2002 and is seen here at its depot on 5 March 2003. (K. A. Jenkinson)

New to Arriva Netherlands in April 2002, left-hand drive Wright Commander-bodied DAF SB200 5957 (BN-DS-82) is fitted with a sliding, rather than folding, front door. (Author's collection)

Resting at Groningen, Holland, are Arriva Netherlands Wright Commander-bodied left-hand drive DAF SB200s 5954 (BN-DS-79) and 5975 (BN-HD-81), both of which were new in April 2002. (Author's collection)

Seen at Bluewater is Arriva Kent Thameside twenty-nine-seat Wright Cadet-bodied DAF SB120, which was new in January 2004. (D. W. Rhodes)

Route branded for the 33 service is Travel West Midlands Wrightbus Eclipse Gemini-bodied Volvo B7TL 4483 (BJ03 EWR), which was new in June 2003 and is seen here in Carrs Lane, in Birmingham city centre. (K. A. Jenkinson)

Marketed by Volvo as the Merit, on behalf of Wrightbus, Warrington Borough Transport DAF SB120 38 (DG53 FJX) was purchased new by the municipal operator in October 2003. (M. H. A. Flynn)

Looking immaculate, despite being ten years old, is Translink Ulsterbus Wright Solar-bodied Scania L94UB 757 (TCZ 1757), seen here in Belfast on 29 November 2013. Behind it is Translink Metro 2817 (CCZ 8817), a Wright Renown-bodied Volvo B10BLE dating from December 1999. (Paul Savage)

Kowloon Motor Bus, Hong Kong, AVW22 (LL 3373) is a dual-door, eighty-seat Wright Super Olympian-bodied tri-axle Volvo B10TL which was one of a large batch supplied new in 2004. (Nigel Eadon-Clarke)

Purchased new by Transdev Harrogate & District in February 2004, branded for the prestigious 36 service from Leeds to Ripon, and fitted with sixty-eight coach seats, is Wright Eclipse Gemini-bodied Volvo B7TL 3610 (YC53 MXY). It is seen here in Harrogate on 20 April 2010. (K. A. Jenkinson)

Resting in Buxton Market Place on 6 October 2019 is High Peak Bus Co. Wright Solar-bodied Scania L94UB 693 (FN04 HTU), which began life with Trent in May 2004. High Peak is a company jointly owned by Bowers, Chapel-en-le-Frith, and Trent. (K. A. Jenkinson)

Collecting its passengers in Whitehall Street, in its home city, on 18 February 2006, is Travel Dundee's Wright Eclipse Gemini-bodied Volvo B7TL 13 (SP54 CGY), which was new in October 2004. (Murdoch Currie)

Wearing branding for route 33, and seen here standing in Cannock bus station, is Arriva Midlands North thirty-seat Wright Cadet-bodied VDL SB120 2702 (YJ54 CKF), which started life in November 2004. (K. A. Jenkinson)

Seen in Guildford bus station, painted in a dedicated park and ride livery, is Arriva Guildford & West Surrey Wright Eclipse-bodied Volvo B7RLE 3731 (GN54 MYO), which was purchased new in November 2004. (Barry Newsome)

New in May 2005, Kowloon Motor Bus, Hong Kong, Wright dual-door Super Olympian-bodied tri-axle Volvo B10TL AVW76 (LX 9702) is seen here below the mass transit railway on the bridge above. (Nigel Eadon-Clarke)

The first of only four fifty-one-seat Wright Eclipse Commuter-bodied Volvo B7RLEs to be built was Ulsterbus 2201 (WCZ 2201), which was new in April 2004. (Irish Transport Heritage)

Seen in Stratford on 31 July 2012 is Go-Ahead London's dual-door Wright Cadet-bodied VDL SB120 DWL29 (FJ54 ZTX), which was new in September 2004. (K. A. Jenkinson)

Approaching the O2 Arena at North Greenwich is Abellio Wright Eclipse Gemini dual-door-bodied Volvo B7TL 9028 (BX55 XMA), which started life in December 2005 with Travel London. (K. A. Jenkinson)

New to Reading Buses in March 2005, but seen here in Ripon bus station on 25 September 2013 after being purchased by independent Eddie Brown, is Wright Solar-bodied Scania L94UB YN05 GXD. (K. A. Jenkinson)

Bearing all the hallmarks of Wright's design, this 2005 rear-engined Opus midibus, the body of which was supplied by Wright in ckd form, is seen hard at work in Long Beach, California, USA. (Author's collection)

Displaying its Cummins engine, the rear profile of this Capital Metro, Austin, Texas, USA, Opus clearly shows its Wright heritage. (Author's collection)

Supplied new to First Capital, London, in October 2005, was Wright Eclipse Gemini-bodied Volvo B7TL 32657 (LK55 ACO), which has been converted from dual to single-door layout. It is seen here in 2019 after entering preservation and being painted in the old Strathclyde Buses livery. (Richard Walter)

London Central Wright Electrocity WHY3 (LX55 EAE) was new in February 2006 and was fitted with a twenty-six-seat dual-door body. (Author's collection)

Seen at York station, on its first day in service in May 2006, and showing its front wheel covers, which were later removed, is First York Wright ftr-bodied Volvo B7LA bendy bus 19004 (B7 FTR). (K. A. Jenkinson)

New in May 2006, First Northern Ireland 66993 (RKZ 4760) is a dual-door Wright Eclipse Urban-bodied Volvo B7RLE which later crossed the water to join First Somerset & Avon. (Paul Savage)

Arriva West Yorkshire's forty-four-seat Wright Commander-bodied VDL SB2000 1414 (YJ57 BVY), which dates from September 2007, heads through City Square, Leeds, on its journey from Huddersfield on 8 January 2014. (K. A. Jenkinson)

Painted in Fastrack livery, Arriva Kent Thameside 3825 (GN07 AVO), which was new in May 2007, is a forty-one-seat Wright Eclipse Urban-bodied Volvo B7RLE. (D. W. Rhodes)

The first Wright Meridian body to be built was exhibited at the October 2007 Coach & Bus Show at the NEC, Birmingham. Mounted on a MAN NL273F chassis, it was destined to join the fleet of Scottish independent Whitelaw at Stonehouse during the following month. (K. A. Jenkinson)

You wait for one, and three turn up. Three First Leeds Wright ftr-bodied Volvo B7LA bendy buses headed by 19023 (YJ07 LVR), which entered service in March 2007, rest in Eastgate, Leeds, on 7 October 2015 while operating the Hyperlink 72 service to Bradford, for which they are branded. As can be seen, the unsuccessful – and unpopular – front wheel covers have now been removed. (K. A. Jenkinson)

Standing outside dealer Arriva Coach & Bus, Gildersome, on 19 November 2008 when brand new, Wright Pulsar-bodied VDL SB200 2909 (CX58 EWZ) is ready for delivery to its first owner, Arriva Cymru. (K. A. Jenkinson)

New in April 2008, East Yorkshire 743 (YX08 FXE), a Wright Eclipse Gemini 2-bodied Volvo B9TL, leaves York on 8 August 2008 at the start of its long journey to Hull on the X46 service, for which it carries branding. (K. A. Jenkinson)

Ulsterbus 424 (UEZ 2424), which was new in November 2008 and is seen here in Belfast, is a fifty-five-seat Wright Solar Rural-bodied Scania K230UB which features a central, hinged wheelchair access door. (Paul Savage)

Translink Foyle Metro Wright Eclipse Gemini 2-bodied Volvo B9TL 2257 (OEZ 7257), which began life in January 2008, turns into the bus station in its home city, Londonderry. (Paul Savage)

First York's Wright Eclipse Urban-bodied Volvo B7RLE 69361 (YJ08 ZGO), which was new in May 2008, is seen here on 3 October 2019 retrofitted with an advert panel on its roof edge. (K. A. Jenkinson)

Representing the low-height Wright Gemini 2, using an VDL underframe, is Arriva Selby's 1500 (YJ59 BTO), which was new in November 2009. It is seen here leaving York for its hometown. (K. A. Jenkinson)

The integrally built Wrightbus Gemini 2, using VDL underframe components, is illustrated by Arriva London North DW237 (LJ59 AEG), which began life in the capital in September 2009 and is pictured here passing Mansion House. (K. A. Jenkinson)

Seen in Huntingdon on 20 October 2010, while still waiting the long-delayed opening of the Cambridge Guided Busway, is Stagecoach Cambus Wright Eclipse Urban-bodied Volvo B7RLE 21226 (AE09 GYW), which was new in April 2009. It had still to be fitted with its guide wheels. (K. A. Jenkinson)

Two of SBS Transit Singapore's dual-door Wright Eclipse Gemini 2-bodied tri-axle Volvo B9TLs, SBS 3321E and SBS 3328L, which were new in 2012, are seen here in their sunny native surrounds. (Author's collection)

New in February 2011, displaying Dynamo branding below its cab window, is First Leeds Wright Eclipse Gemini 2-bodied Hybrid Volvo B5LH 39201 (BJ06 BZA), seen here on demonstration to the media on 23 March 2011. (K. A. Jenkinson)

Originally registered OU09 EAW when new to Weardale Motor Services, Stanhope, in April 2009, Wright Meridian-bodied MAN NL273F W666 WMS is seen here at Plaxton's dealership yard at Anston, hopeful of finding a new owner after its sale by Weardale. (Plaxton)

Passing through Enniskillen, on 9 April 2016, is Ulsterbus 192 (AFZ 1192), a Wright Eclipse SchoolRun-bodied Volvo B7R which was new in February 2010. (Paul Savage)

Seen in Northern Ireland in April 2010 before being delivered to Kowloon Motor Bus, Hong Kong, is unregistered Wright Super Olympian-bodied tri-axle Volvo B9TL AVBWU6 (PH 4712). (Paul Savage)

Displayed at the November 2010 Euro Bus Expo show at the NEC, Birmingham, is this Wright Eclipse Gemini 2-bodied hybrid Volvo B5LH. (K. A. Jenkinson)

New in June 2011, and seen here heading to Bury, is Maytree of Bolton's thirty-seven-seat Wrightbus StreetLite WF MX11 EGV. (M. H. A. Flynn)

Carrying Hybrid Electric Bus promotional lettering and route branding on its side panels is Bullock of Cheadle's Wright Eclipse Gemini 2-bodied Volvo B5LH BU11 OCX. It is seen here when it was new in March 2011. (Volvo)

Seen in Londonderry, on 29 September 2015, is Ulsterbus Foyle 500 (EFZ 9500), a fifty-five-seat Wright Solar Rural bodied Scania K230UB which was new in March 2011. (Paul Savage)

Seen in the yard of Dawsonrentals (dealer) in December 2019 carrying fictitious registration and fleet numbers BU12 HHJ and MN 0123, this mock-up of a Wrightbus New Bus for London had no mechanical units or upper deck interior fittings. (Author's collection)

Looking immaculate and branded for the Cymru Coastliner service is Arriva Cymru's low-height integrally built Wrightbus Gemini 2 4481 (CX61 CDE), which was new in February 2012. (Author's collection)

Painted in a special livery and being used in Belfast in 2012 as part of the Olympic torch relay is Stagecoach Red & White Wrightbus StreetLite WF 43007 (CN12 ASO). (Paul Savage)

Displayed on the Wrightbus stand at the Euro Bus Expo show at the NEC in November 2012 is Arriva Yorkshire's Pulsar 2-bodied Euro 5-engined VDL SB200 1495 (YJ62 JMX). (K. A. Jenkinson)

Chassis are seen here being assembled at Wright's EN-Drive factory in Antrim in 2014. (EN-Drive)

Pictured here on trade plates being road-tested near the Cummins factory in Darlington is Wrightbus's New Bus for London development vehicle. (Author's collection)

Seen near the Olympic Park at Stratford, in July 2012, is London Borough of Redbridge's forty-four-seat Nu-Track-bodied Mercedes Benz 1524L LL11 XPT, which was new in August 2011. (K. A. Jenkinson)

Caught by the camera in Hackney, London, on 22 March 2012 when only a few weeks old, is Arriva London North Wrightbus New Bus for London LT2 (LT61 BHT). (K. A. Jenkinson)

Seen on the same day as the previous photograph, albeit at Hyde Park Corner, London, Wrightbus's New Bus for London, LT2 (LT61 BHT), shows off its open rear door as it heads for its route 38 journey's end at Victoria. (K. A. Jenkinson)

Fitted with a dual-door Wrightbus Eclipse Gemini body, Dublin Bus Volvo B9TL GT43 (12-D-38790), which was new in October 2012, passes through Parnell Square, Dublin, in August 2016. (Paul Savage)

Minibuses being built in Nu-Track's Antrim factory. (Nu-Track)

Loaned to First West Yorkshire for a few months in the autumn of 2014 for evaluation was Transport for London (Arriva London North) Wrightbus New Bus for London LT2 (LT61 BHT), which was repainted green and given First logos. It is seen here at First Bradford's depot on 7 August of that year. (K. A. Jenkinson)

Fitted with a Wrightbus Gemini 3 body, Arriva West Yorkshire hybrid Volvo B5LH 1711 (YJ13 FKP), which was new in March 2013, is seen here in Leeds when only a few weeks old. It is adorned with promotional hybrid-electric lettering above and below its lower deck windows. (K. A. Jenkinson)

Fitted with a forty-five-seat Nu-Track-Merlyn body, Mercedes Benz Atego 1623L RHZ 2720 was supplied new to Western Education and Library Board, Omagh, Ulster, in July 2013. (Nu-Track)

Collecting its passengers in Ripon bus station, on 25 September 2013, is Dales & District (Leeming Bar) Wrightbus StreetLite WF MX62 GUG, which was new in January of that year. (K. A. Jenkinson)

New to First Capital, London, in May 2013, WSH62996 (LJ13 JWP) was a zero emission thirty-four-seat dual-door Wrightbus Hydrogen Fuel Cell Electrocity. (Wrightbus)

In November 2013, Arriva the Shires introduced eight battery electric thirty-seven-seat Wrightbus StreetLite WF EVs with underfloor inductive charging. One of these, 5003 (KP63 TDX), is seen here in Bletchley bus station a few months after entering service. (K. A. Jenkinson)

Showing the revised front fitted to Wrightbus's Eclipse Urban, and its emergency exit in the centre of its offside rather than behind its rear axle, is First Halifax Volvo B7RLE 69584 (BT13 YWA), which began life with First South Yorkshire in November 2013. (K. A. Jenkinson)

Built by Wrightbus and based on the StreetLite WF but sold in left-hand drive format as the VDL Citea MLE, this example was supplied new to Nobina, Denmark, in December 2014. (Author's collection)

Displayed on the Wrightbus stand at the Euro Bus Expo show, at the NEC in November 2014, was this hybrid electric StreetLite WF EV. (K. A. Jenkinson)

Seen at Stratford in July 2012, while on loan for the London Olympics, Thamesdown Wrightbus StreetLite DF 414 (WX12 GDV), which was new a couple of weeks earlier, shows the extra ventilation panels above its offside windows. (K. A. Jenkinson)

On display at the Irish Transport Trust Bus & Coach Rally at Cultra, Co. Down, in April 2013 before delivery to its owner, Go-Ahead London General, is dual-door Wrightbus StreetLite DF WS25 (LJ13 GKP). (Paul Savage)

Built as a demonstrator and evaluated by Dublin Bus in March 2014 (registered 141-D-19194), it then passed to Ulsterbus, who numbered it 2040 and re-registered it BX14 SYT. It is a Wrightbus Gemini 3-bodied Volvo B5TL with glazed panels showing its staircase and is seen here in Castle Place, Belfast, on 28 July 2015. After completing its trials in Ulster, it was sold to East Yorkshire Motor Services who gave it fleet number 797. (Paul Savage)

Built by Nu-Track in April 2014, thirty-three-seat Mercedes Benz 0813 FXZ 6512 was delivered new to Southern Education and Library Board, Armagh, in Northern Ireland. (Nu-Track)

Seen in Central London carrying Thames Valley branding is Reading Buses' thirty-five-seat Wrightbus StreetLite DF 167 (SN14 FGP), which was new in June 2014. (Richard Walter)

Immaculately presented in its owner's striking livery is Bournemouth Yellow Buses' Wrightbus Gemini 3-bodied Volvo B5TL VGW192 (BF15 KFA), which was new in March 2015. (M. H. A. Flynn)

Amongst the first integrally built Wrightbus StreetDecks to enter service was Brighton & Hove 929 (BX15 ONF), which featured the original unglazed front upper deck corner pillars. It was new in April 2015 and is seen here wearing Coaster branding for the service from Brighton to Eastbourne. (T. S. Blackman)

Featuring a glazed staircase and unglazed front upper deck corner pillars is Lothian Buses' Wright Gemimi 3 Stealth-bodied Volvo B5TH 427 (SA15 VTE), which was new in June 2015. It is seen here at Edinburgh Airport on 21 March 2017. (Richard Walter)

Xplore Dundee thirty-two-seat Wrightbus StreetLite WF 435 (SN65 OME), which was new in September 2015, is seen here in the city centre in November 2018. It is followed by Wright Eclipse Gemini-bodied Volvo B7TL BU06 CXC, which had begun life with West Midlands Travel in August 2006. (Richard Walter)

Leaving its home city's transport interchange is First Bradford forty-one-seat Wrightbus StreetLite DF 63278 (SL15 ZFH). (K. A. Jenkinson)

Displaying a Nu-Track Wright logo on its bonnet, Nu-Track-bodied Fiat Ducato XFZ 8877 is seen here at the Coach & Bus Live exhibition at the NEC, Birmingham, in September 2015. (K. A. Jenkinson)

Seen leaving the Olympic bus park at Stratford in July 2012 is Arriva London South Wrightbus Pulsar Gemini-bodied VDL DB250 DW107 (LJ05 BKA), which was new in March 2005. It is followed by Metroline Eclipse Gemini-bodied Volvo B9TL VW1292 (LK12 ARO), which had entered service in June 2012. (K. A. Jenkinson)

Collecting its passengers in Chatham bus station is Arriva Kent Thameside low-height Wrightbus StreetDeck 6801 (SL16 YPH), which was new in June 2016 and has unglazed front upper deck corner pillars. (D. W. Rhodes)

Seen arriving at Bradford Transport Interchange, on 3 September 2019, is First Leeds Wrightbus normal-height StreetDeck 35214 (SL16 RFZ), which was new in May 2016. It features unglazed front upper deck corner pillars. (K. A. Jenkinson)

Built in July 2016 as a part open-topper for Edinburgh sightseeing duties and having glazed front upper deck corner pillars, Lothian Buses 234 (SJ16 CTX) is a Wrightbus Eclipse Gemini 3 Stealth-bodied Volvo B5TL. (Richard Walter)

Metroline, London, Wrightbus Gemini 3 Stealth-bodied hybrid Volvo B5LH VWH2190, which was new in August 2016, is seen here branded for route 140. (Author's collection)

Nu-Track thirty-three-seat Nu-Vibe LRZ 3094, which shared some of Wrightbus's StreetLite styling, began life in September 2016 as a demonstrator. (Nu-Track)

Seen here on display at the Euro Bus Expo show at the NEC, Birmingham, when brand new in 2016, is Reading Buses Wrightbus StreetDeck 906 (SK66 HSA). (K. A. Jenkinson)

New in 2016, Metroline VWH2243 (LK66 EOO) was a Wrightbus Gemini 3 Stealth-bodied hybrid Volvo B5LH, with different pillar spacing to accommodate its centre door. It is seen here at an open day at Potters Bar garage. (Nigel Eadon-Clarke)

Exhibited on the Wrightbus stand at the Euro Bus Expo event at the NEC, in November 2016, and branded for the Fastway 100 service, is Metrobus StreetLite DF 6104 (SK66 HSY). (K. A. Jenkinson)

Fitted with a Wrightbus body of the same design as the New Bus for London, but with only two doors, is London Sovereign Volvo B5LH VHR45208 (LJ66 EZU), which was new in November 2016. (Wrightbus)

One of a large number of Wrightbus-bodied Volvo B9TLs supplied to New World First Bus, Hong Kong, 5221 (UL 3677) was new in November 2016. (Author's collection)

The first zero emissions Wrightbus StreetAir EV to be built was twenty-three-seat dual-door LK66GPF, which is seen here in February 2017 before being registered. (Wrightbus)

Seen here when brand new in April 2017 is Translink Ulsterbus Wrightbus Eclipse Gemini 3 Stealth-bodied Volvo B5TL 2100 (FGZ 3100), which is branded for the express service from Belfast city centre to its international airport. (Paul Savage)

Sharing some similarity with Wrightbus's StreetLite WF is Nu-Track's Nu-Vibe, a May 2017 thirty-three-seat example of which, 353 (29090), is seen here. It is operating for CT Guernsey displaying the Wrightbus logo on its front panel. (Author's collection)

Typifying the New Bus for London, and showing its three-door layout, is Go-Ahead London Central LT867 (LTZ 1867), which was new in November 2016. It is seen here en route to Deptford Bridge on the 453 service. (Richard Walter)

D & E Coaches' (Inverness) thirty-seven-seat Wright StreetLite WF SK17 HHG was new in April 2017. It is seen here in its home city on 24 July 2018. (Richard Walter)

Seen in Belfast on its first day in service (12 April 2017) is Translink Metro Wright Eclipse Gemini 3 Stealth-bodied Volvo B5TL 2112 (FGZ 3112). It featured glazed front upper deck corner pillars. (Paul Savage)

Wearing Big Bus branding with part of its livery covering its glazed staircase, Dualway Rathcoole's part open-top Wright Eclipse Gemini 3 Stealth-bodied Volvo B5TL 171-D-41645, which was new in May 2017, is seen in Dublin followed by two Dublin Bus Wright Eclipse Gemini 3-bodied Volvo B5TLs. (Paul Savage)

Featuring a glazed staircase and front upper deck corner pillars, Lothian Buses Wrightbus Eclipse Gemini 3 Stealth-bodied hybrid Volvo B5LH 571 (SJ67 MFE) made its debut in September 2017. (Richard Walter)

One of six Wrightbus twenty-seven-seat StreetAir single-deckers purchased new by Lothian Buses in September 2017 is 286 (SK67FLE), seen here en route to Easter Road on service 1. (Richard Walter)

Sullivan Buses (Potters Bar) SL92 (JJ67 SUL) is a twenty-five-seat Wrightbus dual-door StreetLite DF which was new in December 2017. (Author's collection)

Built in December 2017 as a demonstrator for evaluation by Tower Transit, Singapore, SG 4003D is an eighty-four-seat dual-door Wrightbus Eclipse Gemini 3 Stealth-bodied tri-axle 11.8m Volvo B8L with glazed upper deck front corner pillars. It is seen here in its new home a few days after entering service. (Wrightbus)

Lothian East Coast Buses Wrightbus Eclipse 3 Facelift-bodied Volvo B8RLE 10054 (SF17 VMA), with a Stealth-style windscreen and seen here in Edinburgh, was new in April 2017. (Richard Walter)

Go-Ahead London General VHP2 (BV18 YAE), which was new in June 2018, is a Volvo B5LHC fitted with a pantograph, for current collection, on the roof of its sixty-seat dual-door Wrightbus New Bus for London-style body. (Author's collection)

Resting between duties in Dublin, on 24 November 2018, is Go-Ahead Ireland's Wrightbus Eclipse Gemini 3-bodied Volvo B5TL 11554 (182-D-463), which was new in July 2018. It features an inward-angled windscreen which gives the body a more bulbous frontal appearance. (Paul Savage)

Transdev Yorkshire Coastliner Wrightbus Eclipse Gemini 3 Stealth-bodied Volvo B5TL 3642 (BN68 XPR), which was new in September 2018, looks immaculate as it stands outside York railway station on 3 September 2019. (K. A. Jenkinson)

One of a large number of Wrightbus-bodied tri-axle Volvo B8Ls ordered by Kowloon Motor Bus, Hong Kong, is seen here before delivery in October 2018. (Wrightbus)

Launched in November 2018 as the world's first fuel cell double-decker, the Wrightbus StreetDeck FCEV immediately gained orders from Transport for London (twenty) and First Aberdeen (fifteen). (K. A. Jenkinson)

Seen on public display in its new home is low-height, dual-door, left-hand drive Wrightbus StreetDeck LD JW 32, which was supplied to Buses Vule, Santiago, Chile, in January 2019. (Wrightbus)

Dublin Bus VH1 (192-D-16986), seen here in its home city, is a Wrightbus Eclipse Gemini 3-bodied hybrid Volvo B5LH, which features an inward-angled windscreen and was new in August 2019. (Paul Savage)

The first Wrightbus StreetDeck to be exported to Kowloon Motor Bus, Hong Kong, was W6S1 (WJ 1984), seen here before delivery in September 2019. (Wrightbus)

This example was new to Travel London in December 2005 as a conventional closed-top, dual-door Wright Eclipse Gemini-bodied Volvo B7TL registered BX55 XNB. After being acquired by East Yorkshire and converted to open-top, it was re-registered LF55 CYY and is seen here in Scarborough in July 2019. (D. W. Rhodes)

Showing its roof line and rear profile is Travel London's Wrightbus ElectroCity 8805 (YJ57 YBB), which was new in November 2007. (D. W. Rhodes)

Lothian Country Wright Eclipse Urban-bodied Volvo B7RLE 107 (RIG 6497), which was new to Arriva Kent Thameside in March 2006 (registered GN06 EWD), shows its rear end styling and incorrect B7R badge. (Richard Walter)

Seen at Stratford, London, in July 2012, providing transport for the Olympics, is Go-Ahead London Central Wright Eclipse Gemini-bodied Volvo B7TL WVL272 (LX06 ECF), which was new in March 2006. (K. A. Jenkinson)

Showing Wrightbus's revised Eclipse Gemini 2-styling is Translink Ulsterbus Volvo B9TL 2285 (PEZ 7285), which was new in January 2008. It is seen here at Stratford on London Olympic duties in July 2012 with its owner's identity removed as required by the London Olympic Games Committee. (K. A. Jenkinson)

Fitted with a Wrightbus Eclipse Gemini 2 body with flatter roof, First Games Transport Volvo B9TL 36260 (BG12 YJS), adorned with Shuttle branding, is also seen on London Olympic duties in July 2012 when only a few weeks old. After the Olympics ended, this bus was added to First West Yorkshire's fleet. (K. A. Jenkinson)

Lothian Buses Volvo B5L 590 (SJ67 MHF), which was new in September 2017, illustrates the rear profile of the Wrightbus Gemini 3 Stealth body. (Richard Walter)

Thamesdown Wrightbus StreetLite DF 412 (WX12 GDZ), which was new in June 2012, shows its rear profile while providing games transport at the London Olympics in July 2012. (K. A. Jenkinson)

Seen being demonstrated in St Gallen, Switzerland, is this hybrid, right-hand drive Wrightbus Streetlite WF EV with Electrocity lettering on its side panels. (Wrightbus)

This aerial view shows Wrightbus's Galgorm factory at Ballymena. (Wrightbus)

An internal view of Wrightbus's Ballymena factory in 2019. (Author's collection)

Wearing Ulsterbus Urby branding, Wrightbus StreetDeck 3156 (NGZ 1156), which was new in April 2019 and features a glazed staircase and front upper deck corner pillars, crosses Donegall Quay while operating a school bus duty. (Paul Savage)

Although it was displayed at the Euro Bus Expo show at the NEC, Birmingham, in November 2018, it was not until November 2019 that Translink Belfast Metro put hybrid Wrightbus StreetDeck HEV96 5000 (MXZ 6200) into service. Here it is seen in Belfast city centre a few days after making its debut. (Paul Savage)

Seen before entering service in Hong Kong in December 2019 is Citybus Wrightbus Gemini 3 Stealth-bodied Volvo B8L 8806 (WM 5165). (Author's collection)

Amongst the last buses to leave the Wrightbus factory before it went into administration was Bus Eireann Eclipse Gemini 3 Stealth-bodied Volvo B5TL VWD440, seen here. (Author's collection)

Part of a large order for First Leeds City caught up in the Wrightbus administration saga, StreetDeck 35582 (SK19 EZC), seen here on Galloway Lane, Pudsey, on 12 December 2019, has glazed upper deck front corner pillars. (K. A. Jenkinson)